MW00700627
WONDER
BODY
a sophisticated coloring book
for curious adults
and more
Designed and Illustrated by
Amy Butcher
&
Written by
Alex Jade
another Body Trust project

Printed in the United States of America

Wonder Body:
A Sophisticated Coloring Book for Curious Adults
ISBN: 978-0-9852075-1-9

Got G'nads Press
2261 Market Street #80
San Francisco, CA 94114

www.wonderbody.us

Set in Palatino and Gill Sans using Adobe InDesign
Cover design and illustrations by Amy Butcher
Text by Alex Jade
Author photo © 2017 Zaedryn Sinclair

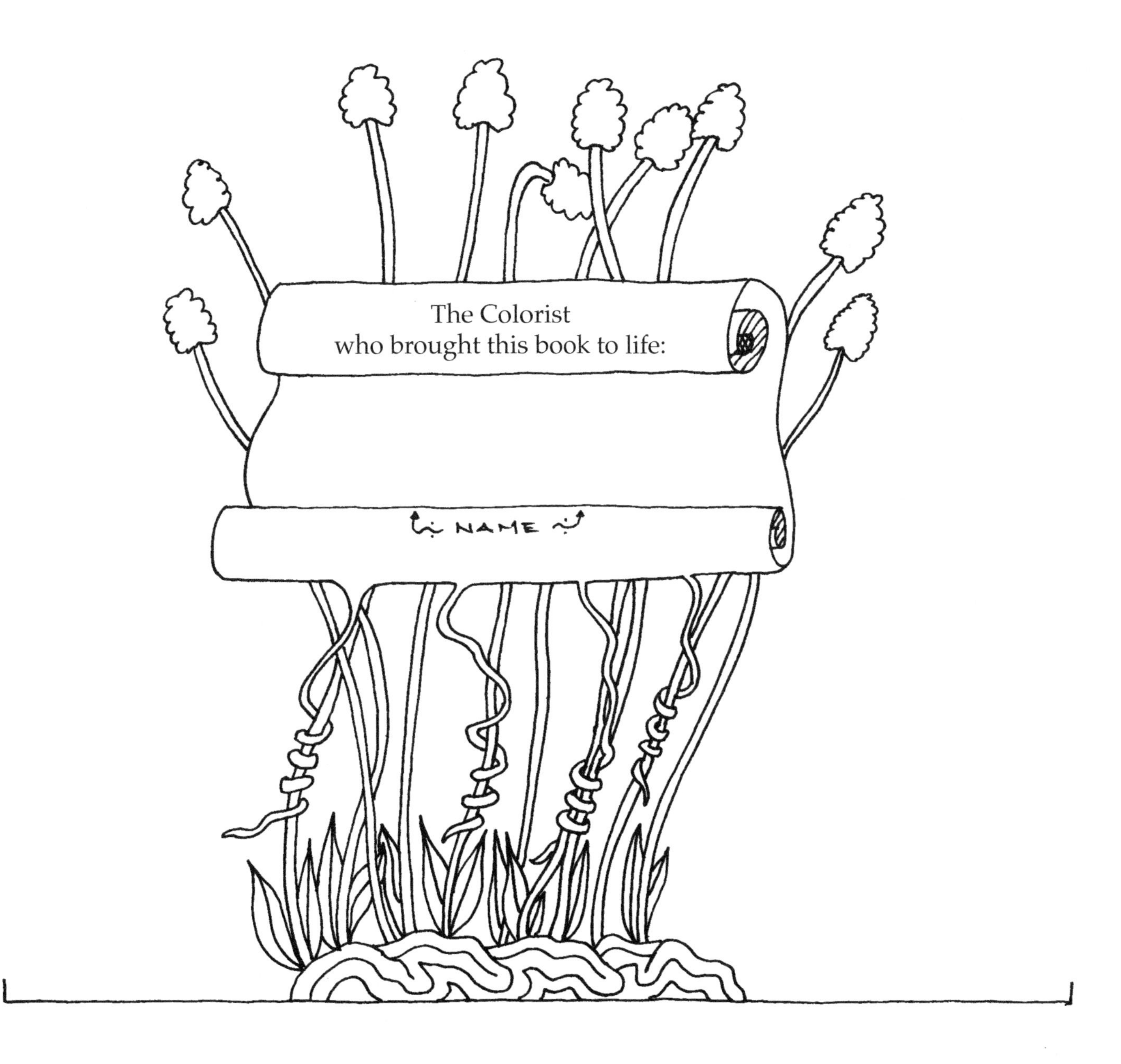

The Colorist
who brought this book to life:
NAME

Wonder Body? What's this all about?

This is beyond a user's guide—it is an experiential owner's manual diving into the pleasure capacities of our bodies. Blending elements of science, body awareness, and creativity, *Wonder Body* hopes to awaken your somatic multi-dimensional capacities. Together—as writer, illustrator, and colorist—we will take a journey from black & white to Technicolor.

Explore of the senses: Did you know there are more than five senses? Way more! Identify and savor fifteen senses in your sensate pleasure body.

Map the subtle energies of the chakra system: Exciting and intriguing, this map of energy in the body, developed in India roughly 3,000 years ago, has no equivalent understanding in allopathic medicine. So we'll use a subtler methodology, channeling an imagined voice of each chakra.

Experience Pleasure: We offer ten other sources of pleasure for your consideration. We all fall into habits that narrow our expectations of what might be pleasurable in the body. Utilize these as an invitation into serendipity and surprise—perhaps you'll expand your pleasure repertoire.

Join the circle: Your engagement with this book may encourage some of the physiological benefits of coloring as a mindfulness practice: decreased cortisol and stress levels, increased immune system function, and a general sense of relaxation. But there is another type of magical alchemy that can happen here, too—circle technology. When two or more are gathered, the third element appears: the group body, the collective energy. It is greater than the sum of the parts. On these pages we have constructed a playground for you filled with visual swingsets and word-based seesaws. But that playground only comes alive when you, the "colorist," come play with us. When you do, we form a circle that feeds us all with creativity, consciousness, connection, and a sense of shared wonder at these magical, malleable bodies in which we live.

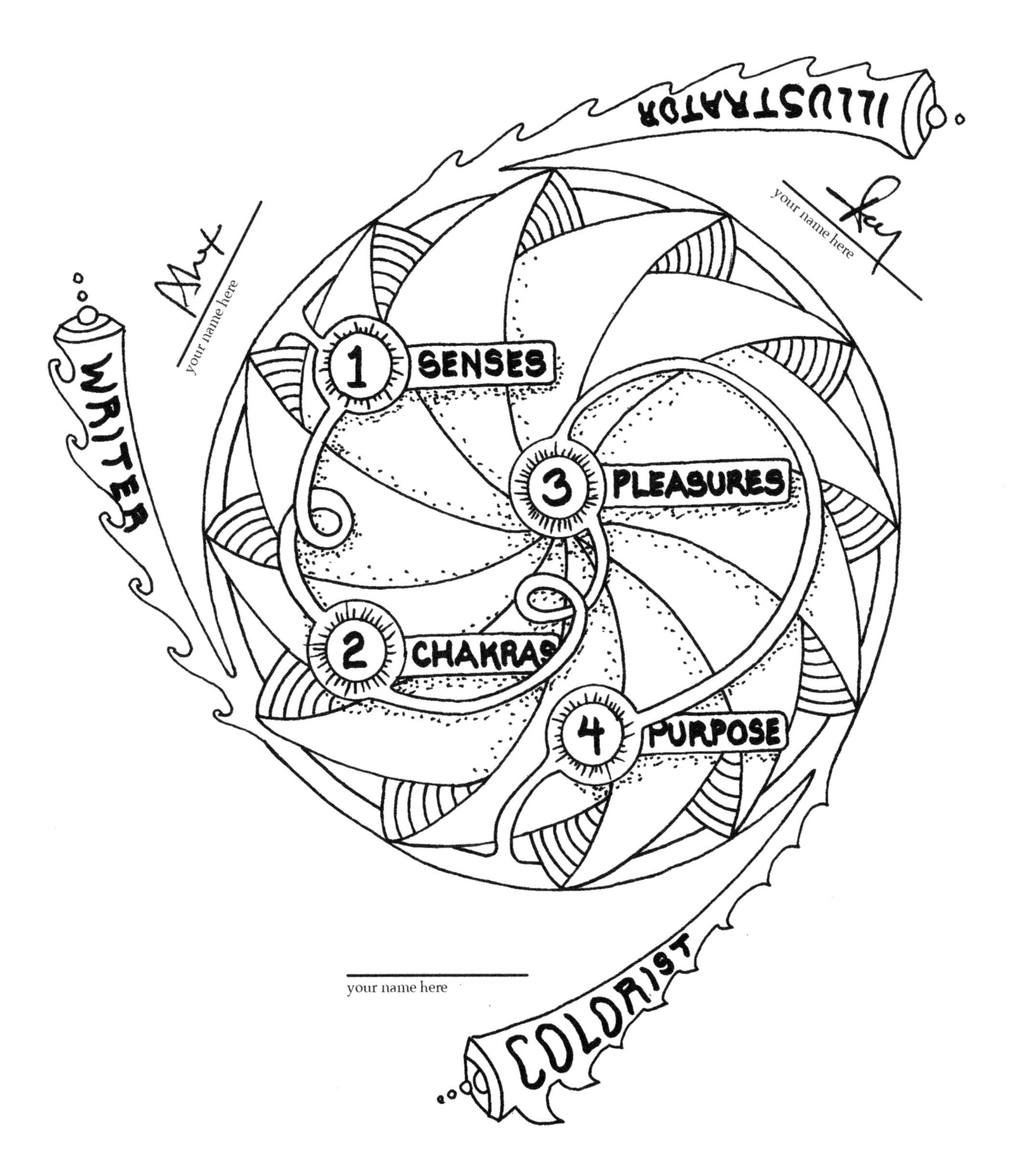
ILLUSTRATOR
your name here
WRITER
your name here
1 SENSES
3 PLEASURES
2 CHAKRAS
4 PURPOSE
your name here
COLORIST

Can you count them on one hand?

Dr. Robert Lawrence, co-founder with Dr. Carol Queen of the Center for Sex & Culture in San Francisco, gives a wildly entertaining lecture on the **20-plus erotically charged sensory systems in our bodies**. As he points out, we are not limited to the big five (sight, smell, taste, touch, hearing) but, in fact, there are many more. Muscles, joints, fascia, and skin hold a wealth of specialized receptors. There are sensory receptors whose job is to feel vibration. Itch is a sense different from pain. Our muscles have Golgi tendon organs to sense tension, muscle spindles to sense stretch. Any one of these might become a source of pleasure—or not.

Robert's list includes: **smell, taste, touch, sight, hearing,** as well as **stretch, temperature, pain, light, itch, rotation, acceleration, proprioception,** and **vibration**. As he points out, this opens up a whole world of sensory pleasures. For example, you might enjoy roller coasters because they engage your sense of acceleration. Or perhaps part of the pleasure of being suspended in midair is in the stimulation of those muscle spindles and Golgi tendon organs. Many erotic pleasures can become uniquely wired. Knowing there are so many more sensory organs available opens up a whole world of new pleasure possibilities.

Let's start with scientific inquiry as a beginning point to understand our senses and the complexity of our bodies. Physiology explores the body and its functions. Physics articulates the process involved in hearing, vision, and sensory receptors. Chemistry comes into play in understanding our nourishment, blood, and nerves. Even ecology sheds light on our interdependence with other beings in this world we occupy and it points out where the forms of the natural world and those of our body mirror each other in a complex ecological dance.

Sensory Systems of the Body

Sense: Sight

The mechanics of sight explain that electromagnetic energy comes in contact with photosensitive cells in our eyes, illuminating, refracting, and reflecting images and colors. Humans develop vision and perception side by side.

It seems like magic. Is it supernatural, or is it mysterious sleight of hand?

Eyes have two specialized sensory receptors: cones and rods. Cones are the photoreceptors in our eyes that can perceive color. Some eyes can see less red or green tones, and others can see an array of color that most mammals can't perceive. The rods are the photoreceptors that see black and white. Rods require less light, so night vision is comprised of rods, which means our eyes can't see color at night. How much light is needed for you to see color? Follow the changing light of dawn and notice when color appears.

Color is sensation, soothing and stimulating.

To gaze is a process of putting full visual attention to an object, like the gaze of an infant seeking contact and reflection. When being gazed upon, the subject responds—is the attention desired or intrusive? Making eye contact can reveal, or it can shield.

Sight

Sense: Smell

"Etymologically speaking, a breath is not neutral or bland—it's cooked air; *we live in a constant simmering. There is a furnace in our cells, and when we breathe we pass the world through our bodies, brew it lightly, and turn it loose again, gently altered for having known us."*

– Diane Ackerman, *A Natural History of the Senses*

Breathing feeds our cells and brings us smells.

In order to smell something, the scent must be in vapor form. Between playing with gravity and the strong pull of inhalation, the vapor can move into our noses. Small channels called turbinates lift moistened air to the yellow olfactory epithelium (specialized tissues with smell receptors) which the air passes on its way into the lungs.

Gagging, coughing, and sneezing expels the irritant that warns of danger. Salivation and gurgling stomach are welcoming invitations. Scent connects to safety, survival, and comfort, becoming a primal conversation with the world and our body.

Flavor and smell go together. If you take away our smell, does chocolate taste different than strawberries?

SMELL

Sense: Taste

Pray at mealtime. Feel gratitude for nourishment.

The mouth is an entry point for the nourishment we take into our bodies. Taste buds are chemical receptors, sensing sour, sweet, salty, bitter, and umami. Mix this with our sense of smell, and we discern the pleasurable, edible, or unsuitable. Saliva moistens food and begins to break down starch, preparing the food to feed us.

People who have more taste buds, called Supertasters, have the capacity to differentiate the breadth of bitter and spicy tones of taste—of which the majority of us have no awareness. Sometimes this is a gastronomic gift; at other times, food can be a source of challenge if it doesn't taste right. Those with fewer taste buds may have less alimentary limits.

Tasting can lead to deeper pleasures, as food is our bodies' nourishment. Sharing food, gifting food, and preparing food with loving attention can become prayer, gratitude, and celebration. The food itself, and our interactions with it, can be medicine.

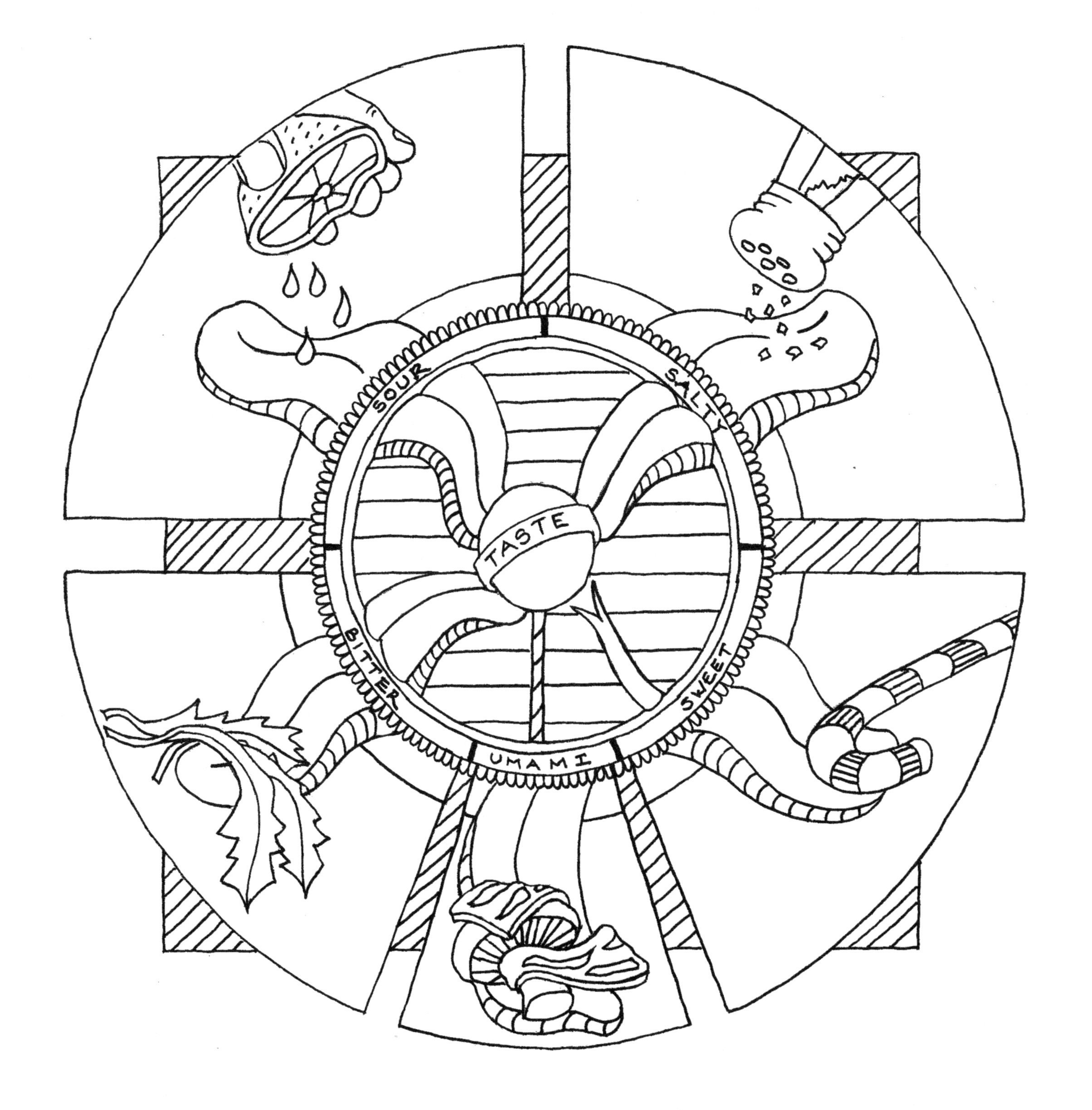
TASTE
SOUR
SALTY
BITTER
SWEET
UMAMI

Sense: Touch

Touch has qualities that can be called light, deep, and sustained. Once there is some kind of touch, the body will send more blood to the surrounding area to investigate. The hairless areas of our fingertips, soles of feet, nipples, and genitals are loaded with Meissner's corpuscles, and they discriminate types of touch. They are zones that are receptors for light touch, and of sensorial receptivity.

Each spinal nerve has a pathway called a dermatome, spreading touch through a map of sensation in the body. Dermatomes light up adjacent dermatomes, alerting and curious. Light touch starting at the little finger and moving along the underside of the arm toward the armpit will send inquisitive impulses along the nerve net to tissues ready to receive sensation.

Skin covers our entire body, and is our largest organ. It is an organ of excretion, a protective covering, and a sensorial banquet. Keratin is the protein that allows skin to be waterproof. Skin tissues are self-healing. Our skin has holes going from the outside to the inside of our bodies, and we have mucus membranes that are packed with a multitude of sensory receptors. Wetness in the mucus membranes is an immune system defense.

If someone reaches out and touches your leg with a hand, can you feel your leg where you are touched, or can you feel the hand touching you? Passively receiving touch is to receive without echoing back to the touch-giver. Actively receiving touch engages both giver and receiver in a response cycle.

Receiving touch is essential to our neurological development. Long hand strokes expanding from head to toe, crossing joints and torso creates a flourishing and responsive brain. Hands and lips can be an offering: soothing, stimulating, and pleasuring. Hugs support, contain, and are a calm harbor to settle into—a primitive statement of interdependence.

TOUCH

Sense: Hearing

"The word 'poet' comes from an Aramaic word that denotes the sound of water flowing over pebbles."

– Diane Ackerman, *A Natural History of the Senses*

Sound waves begin with an action or movement. Waves travel through solids, liquids, or gases and are received by receptors in our ears. Tympanic membranes vibrate and transfer the sound energy to small bones.

The ear bones sound like ancient tools: hammer, anvil, stirrup. Deep inside the ear, the vibrating bones pulse against the oval window of the cochlea, initiating ripples in the fluid which creates force that pulls on the tiny hair cells. These hair cells stimulate neurons sending impulses to the brain. The brain interprets these impulses.

By listening, we keep track of planetary life.

Put an ear to the ground, to wood, to the water. Listen.

We hear sounds within a frequency range of 20-20,000 waves per second, but other animals have different ranges. Bats hear high frequency and use echolocation to move. The crack of a bullwhip is a sonic boom: the tip moves faster than the speed of sound. For us, the earth's movement is too slow to hear with our ears, but perhaps we can "hear" it other ways.

We humans are mammals, and mammals, when in the womb, hear the heartbeat and internal body sounds of our mothers. Sounds can soothe or stimulate our emotions. We emit a myriad of sounds—like speaking, singing, and moaning.

Echo is reflection of sound. Emit a sound, and it will come back to you.

G
I
N
R
A
E
H

Sense: Vibration

"The profound and stable sacred tremor can be reached in extreme states: anger, intense joy, mental wandering or the drive toward survival."

– D. Odier, *Yoga Spandakarika*

A multi-dimensional inquiry. It could be an oscillation, wave, tremor, hertz, frequency, quiver, heartbeat, bright wiggle, or electric charge jiggling. The social statement, "I like your energy," has emotional amplitude, creating a good vibration. Vibration is a primordial starting point, a big blast, the beginning. Vibration is arousal, movement, communication.

Electromagnetic waves have a range of frequencies—physics of light-making color—making color. A way to sense with our skin and eyes simultaneously.

Acoustics, language, sound waves, mechanical motion in a medium, oscillations in our ears—they all vibrate through our skin, muscles, and fascia. So too do earthquakes and rumbling movements that are felt in our bodies. Each chakra has a Sanskrit seed sound, like "Om," which is the sound vibration of our sixth chakra, the Aramaic prayer spreading through time. Adding sound vibration to a chakra can be stimulating, calming, invigorating, soothing, and can be used for meditation or connection.

Skin receptors for flutter and vibration adapt quickly. Sometimes when there is vibration, our pain receptors take a backseat and listen only to that sensation. Some say that using an electric vibration for arousal will shift our body's capacity to feel other types of stimulation. But we only need to remind the sensory receptors of other types of touch—light or deep—in order to experience variety.

Sense: Itch

Itch receptors are located in the skin, and stimulated by a number of chemicals. Most notable is histamine, released in response to cell injury or allergic reaction.

Scratching an itch can be very pleasurable, though the pleasure may be short-lived. Feeling an itch produces strong desire to "do something." Itching is an efficient way of removing insects from the skin.

Why is scratching so pleasurable? Itch and scratch are wed in a sensate and mental process of motivation and reward. Can scratch be satisfying without itch?

Itch

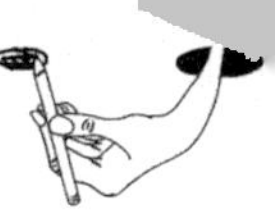

Sense: Temperature

Temperature is a continuum, cold to hot and all in between.

Warm-blooded animals keep a stable body temperature. Humans do this through sensing hot and cold, and stabilizing through body heat regulation. We are a flexible system of regulators—sometimes we put on a coat, pull the covers over us, get close to another body, sit in the shade, or jump in the lake as efforts to keep a thermal homeostasis.

Reptiles and bugs regulate their body temperature through their environments. Honey bees regulate through the hive.

In our skin, including our mucus membranes, we have free nerve endings that detect our unique temperature settings. Our body temperature usually remains around 37°C (98.6°F). Our sensory receptors report "neutral" temperature somewhere between 30–36°C (86–97°F). This is the temperature experienced as "lukewarm" (not cool or warm) when running water over our wrists. When an object touches our skin, in order to protect us and maintain stable body temperature, the temperature nerve endings may report "cold" anywhere within the range of 10–36°C (50–97°F) or "hot" within the range of 32–48°C (90–118°F). Temperatures outside of these ranges are interpreted as potentially damaging to the tissues and picked up by other sensory receptors (i.e., pain) to alert our systems to cellular danger. Ice placed on an injury can be felt as tingling and numbing, acting as an analgesic and slowing inflammation.

Thermoreceptors engage full-body responses. A shiver is a signal of cold, excitement, or fear. Shivering skeletal muscles produce heat and prepare us for action. Cold to our skin sets off a process of constricting blood vessels and increasing metabolic rate, so that warmth protects our core. Blushing, flushing, sweating indicate heat with the desire for cooling. Cold plunges, steam baths, and saunas use external temperature for tuning and healing.

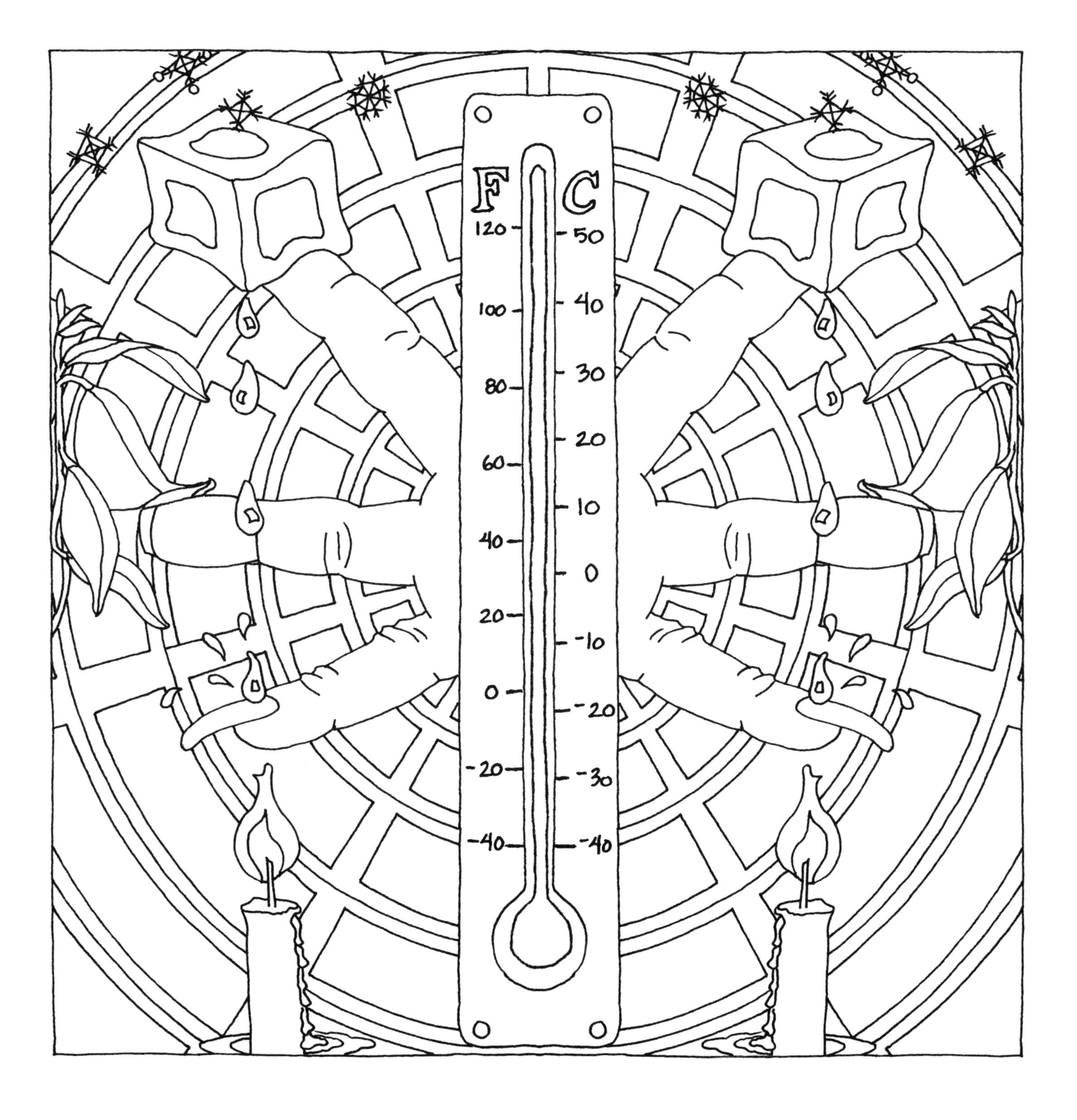
F
C
120
100
80
60
40
20
0
-20
-40
50
40
30
20
10
0
-10
-20
-30
-40

Sense: Pain

Sensation that we call pain is a complex stew of body cell experience and perception. Is pain good or bad?

There are different kinds of pain, with a multitude of ways that we can experience it: high or low temperature, strong pressure to the skin, pricking, pinching, cuts, and blows create a stimulus of cellular action and sometimes an automatic reflex. These sensations may come with riding a bike, picking blackberries, climbing a tree, playing soccer, and being erotic. Bold sensations can be exhilarating, physically strengthening, and liberating. Rupture, cutting, or smashing tissue results in a chemical release, creating a chain of responses to protect the tissue and self heal.

The brain and spinal cord release opioids, our bodies' pain relievers.

Then, there are life threatening kinds of pain, the kinds that are dangerous to our body integrity. Or the aching pain from deep inflammation. Temporary or permanent and woven with emotion, these kinds of pain can cause a changing sense of self, or loss of activity, safety, and capacity.

Our bodies and psyche induce mending after change and / or loss. Healing can take place through many modes: medical intervention, community recognition, prayer, touch, orgasm, or all combined. Give leeway for the mending process, slow or spontaneous.

The amygdala, the almond shaped part of our brain, processes emotion and doesn't discriminate between emotional and physical pain.

But pain is subjective. Who's to say what hurts?

WHO KNOWS YOUR PAIN ?
HOW DO YOU FEEL PAIN ?

Sense: Light

Sunlight is essential for all living organisms.

Photosynthesis in plants is light energy converted to carbohydrates, then into food for insects, animals, and eventually the soil. Light direction and duration promotes the plant growth cycle. Plants turn toward the light. Sunflowers are harbingers of autumn. The diminishing light sends plants into dormancy, an expression of the daylight and night rhythm.

For mammals, light and dark rhythm creates the circadian flow in a roughly 24-hour period: sleep, dream, wake, hunger, contented wellbeing, activity, hormone regulation, slowing down, moving into sleep.

Light receptors in our eyes and skin produce the neurotransmitter serotonin and send information to the pineal gland to produce melatonin—the endocrine system is in flow with the earth cycle. The pineal gland, which is also the 6th chakra, initiates the circadian rhythm.

The pineal gland has been called the third eye, producing insight and inner wisdom. In many lizards and frogs there is a parietal eye, a third eye which is visible; it winks at the daylight and offers a direct route inward. Daylight produces wakeful consciousness; nighttime produces dream-state consciousness.

Luminescent consciousness.

MED
LIGHT
HIGH
LOW

Sense: Proprioception

Proprioception is the felt sense of the periphery, location, and movement of our bodies. *Proprio* means "one's own." This differs from interoception, which is the felt sense of hunger, thirst, emotions, digestion, and other activities that occur within our bodies. Together, proprioception and interoception are embodied awareness.

Proprioception uses touch, muscle movement, tendon stretch with support from balance in the middle ear to sense ourselves in relationship to our environment. These senses are our body geography.

Being aware of our breath is an embodied awareness. The knowledge of your need to take a breath is interoception, the mechanics of breath is proprioception. Breath is body movement, a dance of lungs filling to the movement of diaphragm, ribs, belly, chest, pelvic floor. Breath movement creates depth, width, and length.

Close your eyes and dance. Can you tell where your body is in relation the ground, a window, your nose?

PROPRIOCEPTION

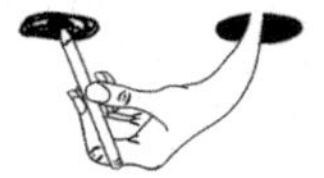

Sense: Stretch

The fibers of our muscles hold the sensory receptors for stretch. Golgi organs monitor tension and are located where the muscle meets the tendon. Muscle spindles in the belly of the muscle detect length and stretch. Golgi organs and muscle spindles explore a unity-dance of support.

Muscle spindles experience stretch and initiate a reflex for the muscles to contract. During a seated meditation, spindles regulate by reflex, adjusting muscles along the spine.

Golgi tendon organs sense muscle tension, and a strong or bold signal will result in a Golgi tendon reflex, with an abrupt relaxation. An arm-wrestling woe occurs when the muscle undergoes tension and there is a quick-release reflex of the loser's arm. It is our reflex protecting muscle, tendon, and bones from tearing.

Stretch receptors are active when receiving deep touch. Touch and movement can be a sensory feast of stretch receptors. There has been little research on the role of stretch receptors in orgasmic response, though it is clear that muscles are active participants: lengthening, tensing, and initiating reflex.

stretch

Sense: Rotation

Rotation can be whirl, turn, spin.

In the inner ear is our vestibular system. The three semicircular canals have receptors that will identify the physical experience of rotation. The canals are at right angles, orthogonal, filled with endolymph fluid interacting with hair, flowing with motion.

When we swirl, are we getting closer to our center through centripetal force or spiritual dynamics? Merry-go-rounds have the calm in the center, and physical excitement moving to the edge.

The drunken "spins." Alcohol-infused blood has thinner properties that confuse the endolymph with density difference, distorting the shape of the hair receptors, creating a phantom movement.

From the North Pole, we can see the Earth rotating counterclockwise (although from the South Pole, it would appear to be rotating clockwise). Most planets, viewed from their North Poles, rotate counterclockwise. Aberrant are Venus and Uranus moving in their own dance with their axes.

Rotation can be in the form of a spiral or helix, movements and forms seen from small to gigantic. The shape of our outer ear, the chakra system, sea shells, nebulas. Look around. Look inside.

ROTATION · ROTATION · ROTATION · ROTATION · ROTATION · ROTATION

Sense: Acceleration

Otoliths are crystals in our inner ear. These calcium carbonate crystals cradled in a viscous gel bump into hair cells. The ear crystals are situated horizontally and vertically. The crystals move, then touch the hairs that have nerve receptors coiled around their bases.

If we hop on a bike or break into a sprint, the crystals move and bend the hair back. Stop suddenly and the crystals jolt forward. Nod your head, ride an elevator, go down a slide—the crystals and hair in the inner ear send signals.

Gravity is a constant force on the crystals, 1g. If we have a change in speed, or accelerate, it takes time for our bodies to adjust to the velocity. The crystals notice when we ride on a motorcycle, get tossed playfully on the bed, and partner-dance.

Physics applies to changes in our body as velocity increases. The pilots of the Blue Angels travel at 700 miles per hour, almost Mach 1, the speed of sound. Most of us would black out.

Are the ear crystals activated when I have a flying dream? Or a falling dream?

Sense: Balance, Equilibrium, and Orientation

Balance is necessary for locating yourself in your environment and moving over varied terrains with curiosity. Body balance uses three sensory systems: vision, proprioception, and the vestibular system—semicircular canals and the otolithic organs. We also need body strength for our equilibrium. As adults, we establish linear routines that numb the sensory pleasures of our vestibular receptors.

As adults, we establish linear routines—walking, working out on gym equipment, sitting at the computer—numbing the sensory pleasures of our vestibular sensory receptors.

Play with your full body . . .

Roll around on a large ball, sit on it and bounce

Climb trees

Jump into water

Go to a playground and swing

Close your eyes and balance on one foot

Use a trampoline

Do a handstand

Practice sun salutations

In the ocean and in space gravitational changes can be disorienting to the vestibular system. The mammals of the ocean have a highly developed sensory system of mineralized mass and sensory hairs, allowing for orientation in three dimensions without gravity or light.

Mapping the Senses

We are in an age of body discovery with new insights emerging about the somatosensory terrain! The scientific understanding and awareness about these systems continues to evolve, even in the last few years.

The first map of the relationship between our brains and our tactile bodies was developed by neurologists in 1950s and was called the sensory homunculus. This map linked our somatosensory sensations to a strip of the cortex in the brain. There were correlations between length of the area on the cortex and the amount of sensory reception at the periphery. Since the hands, feet, face, mouth, tongue had more receptors, they were allotted more corresponding space on the sensory cortex. The discovery continued when maps using MRIs were developed in 2005 to find the location on the cortex for the penis, and in 2011 for the location of the cervix, clitoris, vagina, and nipples.

These mappings and depictions can guide us, but as you can see, the landscape is changing and the maps may be somewhat out of date. How can we become our own brave explorers? We challenge you to birth your own sensorial cartography. Use the coloring pages as a guide or a companion so you can map the truth of your own bodies' responses.

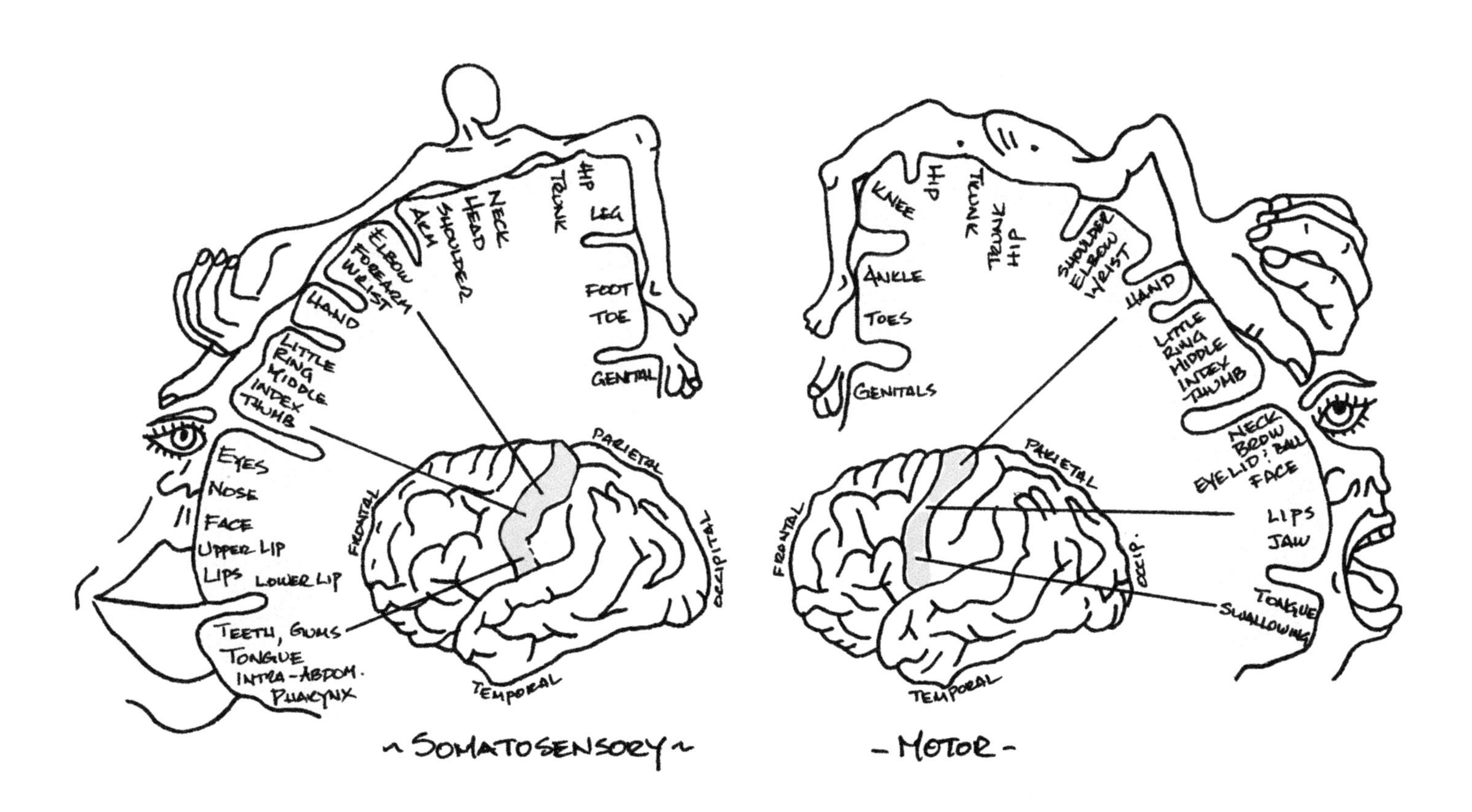
HIP
TRUNK
NECK
HEAD
SHOULDER
ARM
ELBOW
FOREARM
WRIST
LEG
FOOT
TOE
GENITAL
HAND
LITTLE
RING
MIDDLE
INDEX
THUMB
EYES
NOSE
FACE
UPPER LIP
LIPS
LOWER LIP
TEETH, GUMS
TONGUE
INTRA-ABDOM.
PHARYNX
PARIETAL
FRONTAL
OCCIPITAL
TEMPORAL
~ SOMATOSENSORY ~
KNEE
HIP
TRUNK
HIP
ANKLE
TOES
GENITALS
SHOULDER
ELBOW
WRIST
HAND
LITTLE
RING
MIDDLE
INDEX
THUMB
NECK
BROW
EYELID & BALL
FACE
LIPS
JAW
TONGUE
SWALLOWING
PARIETAL
FRONTAL
OCCIP.
TEMPORAL
- MOTOR -

There's more to the body than meets the eye!

The chakra system describes the subtle body system, the energetic rather than material body. Derived from systems of study dating back to 1,500 BC in India, there is no equivalent system of understanding in allopathic medicine, though many indigenous cultures have understandings of an energetic body.

The word "chakra" translates from the Sanskrit to mean wheel or disk. Each can be imagined as an energy vortex where matter and consciousness meet. There are seven main chakras that are aligned with the spine, most extending out of the front and the back of the body. They start at the base of the spine, or root, and run all the way up to the head, or crown.

In addition to describing key elements of each chakra, we've also tried to give each an imaginal voice. What might that chakra say if it could speak to us in words? And how might the energy of each emerge through the conduit of our bodies? What creative spark does each inspire?

The Subtle Energy System

First Chakra: Root

From where I sit, I can see up and down. I am the base of the tail, the coccyx, the focal point, the balance of grounding and support. When I am robust, my tendrils lunge downward, extending toward the ground. Like an umbilical to the planet. A woven web of pelvic fibers holds the form, to tend and support the functions of the entire body.

In fear, I settle in the base of the spine and hold on. I send pulses to my brain, informing the whole body of danger. Sometimes I can't tell when or how to stop holding.

A way I can feel safe is when my anus is held and I feel the movement of breath. When there is an out breath, I move up; an in breath, I move down. In the sea of the body, breath moves me. Tending my anus allows me to be flexible and ready for living.

Come play with me.

Location: Interior of the tailbone, near the perineum
Color: Red
Elemental Sound: Lam
Question: Can I exist?

Second Chakra: Sacral

I am the center of the pulse, feeding from the sensate body. The zeal of creation is my motivation. Flowing and storing, I am the singularly efficient engine of input and output.

Follow the cycle of liquid creation, of drive. What emerges first? Is it the impulse? The desire? Or is it physical function? Impulse is an entry point at the sensate centers, a stir that arouses tissues, ignites an aurora, building the pulse, flooding upward along the spine. When I reach the top, I taste a drop of nectar. Marinating in the flood of my creation, it pools into my reserve.

Location: Interior of the sacrum
Color: Orange
Sound: Vam
Question: Can I create and be generative?

Third Chakra: Solar Plexus

Hot breath. Burning, changing, force. Efficacious combustor, with infinite potential. Flame on. Simple.

Imagine my possibilities: Magic blend of nutrition becoming fuel for tissues. My self-feeding burn of shame. Passionate exchange, building or destroying. Dominance consuming, and submission surrendering.

Turn up the heat, and I am charred wasteland. Turn down the heat, and I am dense, undigested organic material packed into the crevices. Clear vision can guide my flames.

Location: Above the belly button, interior of the spine
Color: Yellow
Sound: Ram
Question: Can I be me?

Fourth Chakra: Heart

I am oxygen and blood. I nurture the whole body. My heart and lungs work as an elegant fuel system, feeding cells blood rich in oxygen, rich in nutrients, rich in feeling. And in the same beat, at the cell level I create the exchange of disposal—cleaning up, purifying, detoxing.

Pumping a tending, nurturing rhythm, which extends outward into the tips of my fingers, lips, toes, genitals, I reach out in offering, and allow receptivity. At the tipping point, the balance crumbles, creating sharp edges of fractured connections. My density and brittleness challenges breath and pulse, straining and constraining. But watch what happens when I turn toward compassion. Try me, and watch.

Returning blood and oxygen. Pumping, feeding, cleaning. Elegant.

Location: Interior of the spine, behind the heart
Color: Green
Sound: Yam
Question: Can I express compassion and unconditional love?

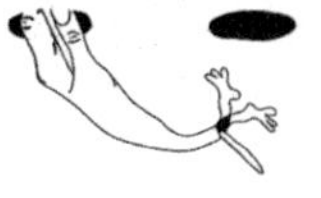

Fifth Chakra: Throat

Enter into the open portal of receiving. Food and breath. I am the paragon of receptivity.

Touch my soft palate: the horizontal surface is a doorway into the inner mind. Or flow down my throat, bifurcating to the belly or lungs. My sound is the sound of breath. When I move in and out, I am the universal mantra.

At the tremor point, I emit ethereal sounds. At the pleasure point, my sounds might be similar, but their meaning is reversed. I create quakes, quivers, moans, lavishing sounds. Vibration. Listening. Constancy.

This moment is art.

Location: Interior of the spine, at the throat
Color: Blue
Sound: Ham
Question: Do I have the will to express myself?

Sixth Chakra: Third Eye

I am the deep seat from which insight emerges. I allow it to rise to the surface, I catch it gently in my palm. My inner-based knowing can be clouded by the unresolved flotsam of my siblings, my confidantes: the lower chakra states and emotions.

When I combine consciousness with alchemy, I transform the constant onslaught of cracks and dross below the diaphragm. I unite us all for a deeper seat. I become a portal, moving beyond time, space, and causality, where I see, I witness, I watch.

Location: Behind the eyes, in the center of the brain
Color: Indigo
Sound: Om
Question: Can I have my vision, and the ability to witness?

Seventh Chakra: Crown

I am so personal, only you and I can know our connection.

Location: Top of the head, cerebral cortex

Color: Purple

Sound: Om, or simply silence

Portals of pleasure!

There is power in pleasure.

Pleasure is an experience of enjoyment, gratification, and fulfillment.

Pleasure can balance, restore, and transform us. It can change us physically, energetically and emotionally. Our bodies are designed for pleasure.

Sometimes there is easy access to pleasure: we find pleasure in the sunlight on our face, enjoying an image or color, or perhaps a kiss. But we can also become numb to our pleasure responses. This detachment can be caused by moods that deflect pleasure, uncomfortable body awarenesses, or painful (emotional or physical) situations. Sometimes, in the moment, we can find balance by drawing awareness to a sensate, mental, or emotional pleasure. Or we can work to build a pleasure reserve to sustain us during a period of pleasure poverty. Erotic energy is our body's pleasure-gold. For most, there is pleasure in touching genitals and other tissues of arousal. But the erotic is a bigger landscape than just that one mother lode and we are more likely to yell "Eureka!" if we expand the scope of our prospecting. The good news is that there are so many possibilities for pleasure all around us, if we can open our sensory systems to them.

The following are ten specific pleasures that Beloveds—the crew of folks who frequently hang out with Body Trust—have told us about. What are some of your quirky pleasures? What allows pleasure to sneak into your being?

For Your Consideration

Pleasure: Citrus Fruit

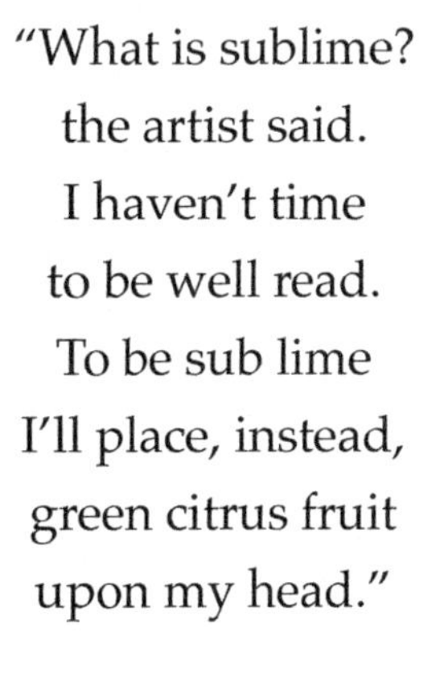

"What is sublime?
the artist said.
I haven't time
to be well read.
To be sub lime
I'll place, instead,
green citrus fruit
upon my head."

– Walter Darby Bannard

Pleasure: Conversation

"The art of
conversation is the
art of hearing
as well as of
being heard."

– William Hazlitt

"I've given guys
blow jobs just because
I've run out of things
to talk about."
"Oh, Rea. Who hasn't?"

– Anne Lamott

"Good communication
is as stimulating as
black coffee
and just
as hard
to sleep
after."

– Anne Morrow Lindberg

CONVERSA-TioN

Pleasure: Curvilinear Spaces

"Music is the expression of the movement of the waters, the play of curves described by changing breezes."

– Claude Debussy

"In life, as in art,
the beautiful
moves in curves."

– Edward G. Bulwer-Lytto

Pleasure: Flowers

"People from a planet
without flowers would think
we must be mad with joy
the whole time to have such
things about us."

– Iris Murdoch

"Nobody sees a flower—
really —it is so small it takes
time—we haven't time—and
to see takes time, like to
have a friend takes time."

– Georgia O'Keeffe

FLOWERS!

Pleasure: “Gross” Things

“As a means of contrast with
the sublime, the grotesque
is, in our view, the richest
source that nature can offer.”

– Victor Hugo

“There is something I
have learned since being
paralyzed, and that is
that in the absence of
sensory information, the
imagination always tends
to the grotesque.”

– Patrick McGrath

“Bleedin’ like a son-of-a-
bitch,” he said. “Well, I can
stop that.” He urinated
on the ground, picked up
a handful of the resulting
mud, and plastered it over
the wound.”

– John Steinbeck

Kombucha
SAUERKRAUT
"GRO
TH NGS"

Pleasure: Ice Cream

"At the end of the day, the argument between spirituality and about spirituality, is all against the nature of spirituality. In arguing spirituality, we go against its very nature. The important question: 'Am I being kind in what I am saying/doing'? And that is all. In all truth, to eat an ice cream cone and to smile with the joy of a child, is about a billion times more spiritual of an activity, than to discuss views about spirituality. The experience of innocence; the experience of joy—this edifies ourselves and others. And that is spirituality. An ice cream cone can be the most spiritual object in the universe, at any given time."

– *C. JoyBell C.*

"Without ice cream, there would be darkness and chaos."

– *Don Kardong*

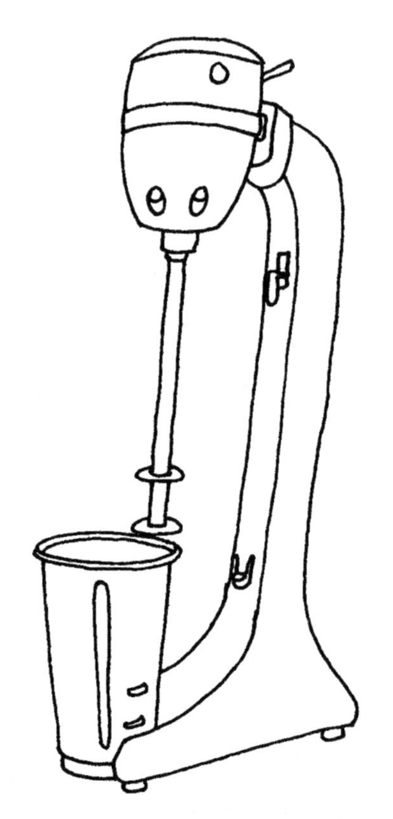

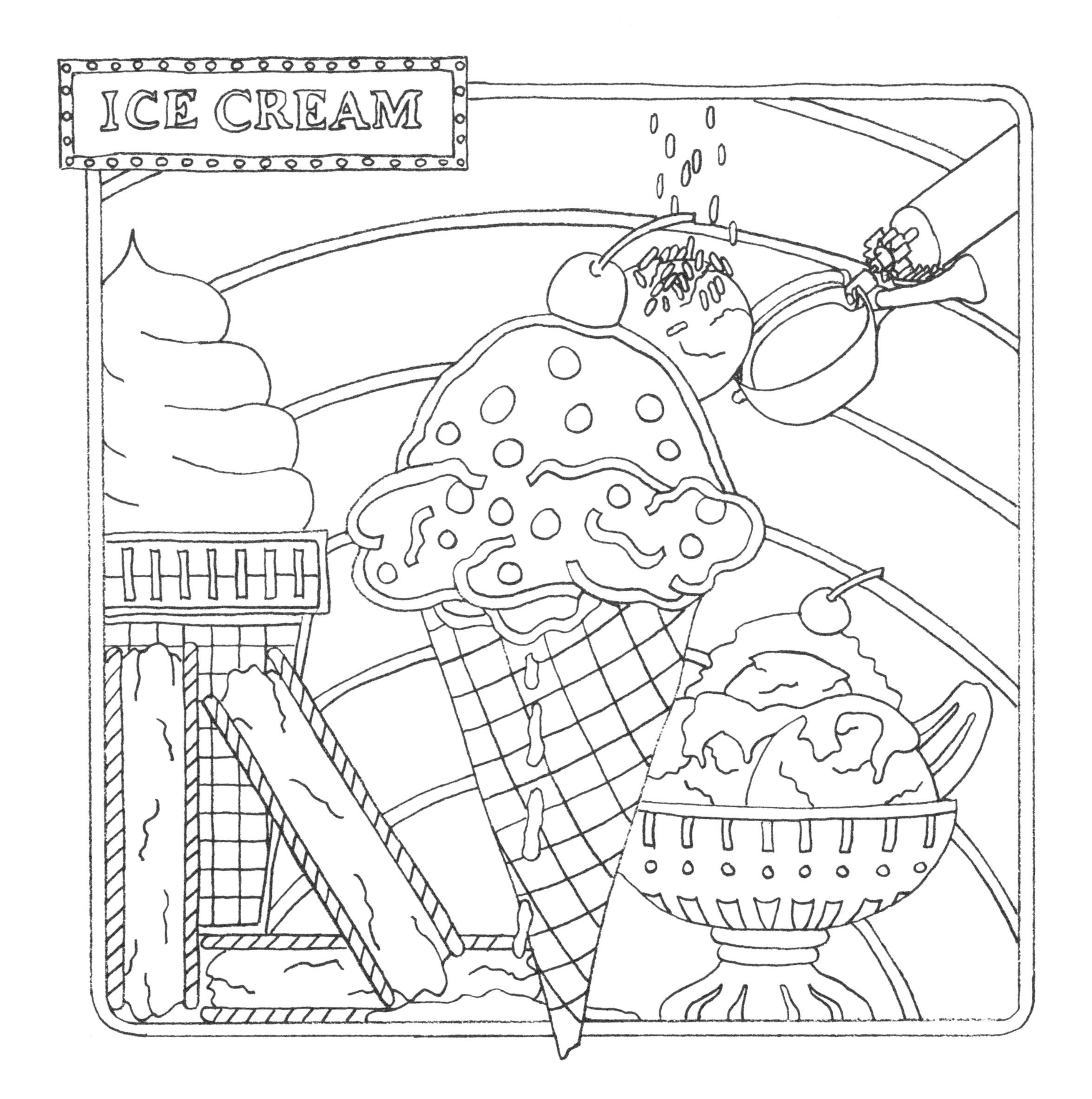
ICE CREAM

Pleasure: Piles of Fall Leaves

"A withered maple leaf has left its
branch and is falling to the ground;
its movements resemble those of a
butterfly in flight. Isn't it strange?
The saddest and deadest of things
is yet so like the gayest and most
vital of creatures?"

– Ivan Turgenev

"Only with a leaf
can I talk of the forest"

– Visar Zhiti

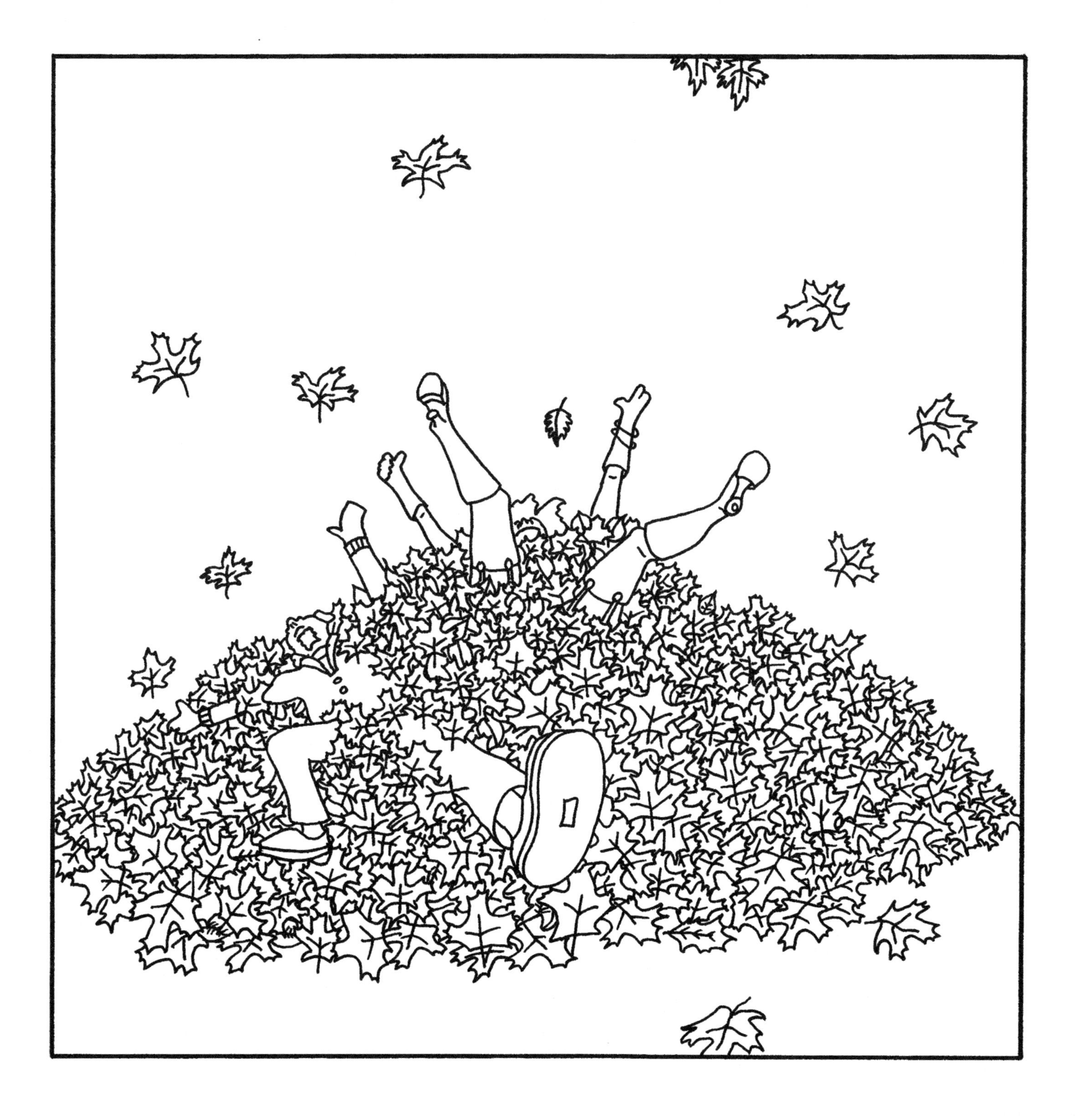

Pleasure: Stationery and Office Supplies

"To the Technocrats: Have mercy on us. Relax a bit, take time out for simple pleasures. For example, the luxuries of electricity, indoor plumbing, central heating, instant electronic communication and such, have taught me to relearn and enjoy the basic human satisfactions of dipping water from a cold clear mountain stream; of building a wood fire in a cast-iron stove; of using long winter nights for making music, making things, making love; of writing long letters, in longhand with a fountain pen, to the few people on this earth I truly care about."

– Edward Abbey

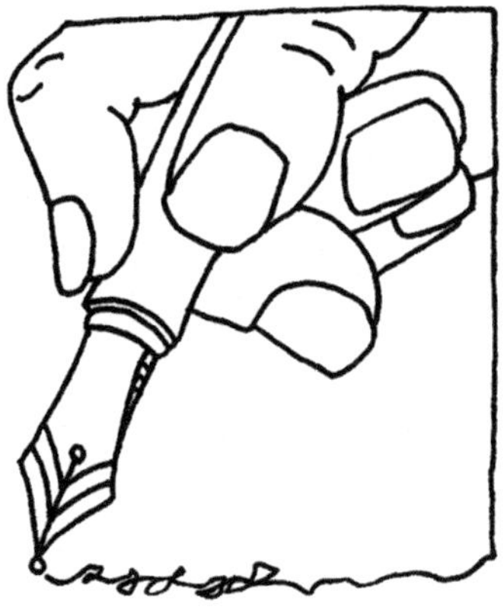

"There had been a problem in Bean's house. The problem was staples. Bean loved staples. She loved them so much that she had stapled things that weren't supposed to be stapled. The things looked better stapled, but her mother didn't think so, and now Bean was outside.

She was going to be outside for a long time."

– Annie Barrows

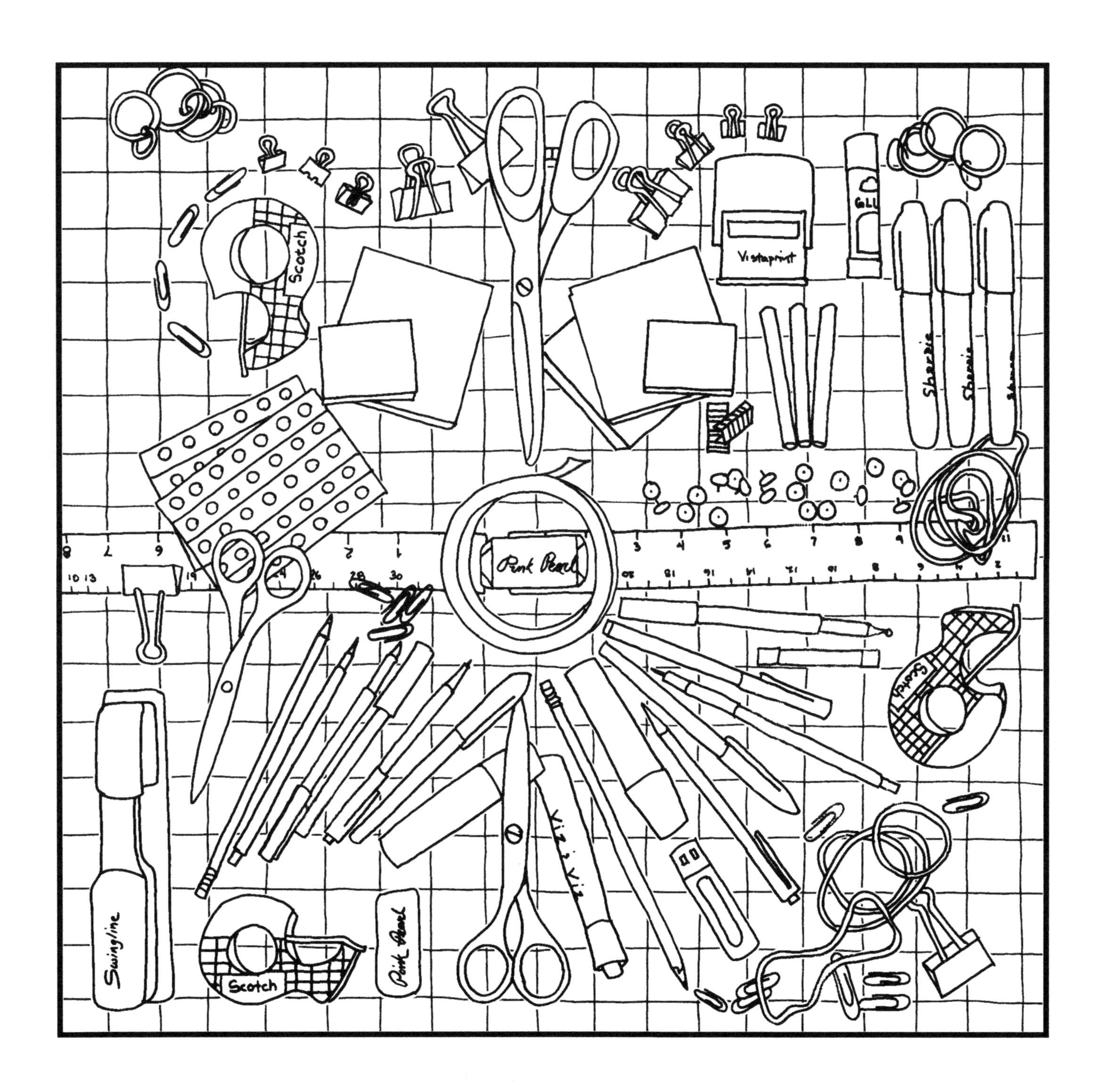
Scotch
Vistaprint
Sharpie
Sharpie
Pink Pearl
Scotch
Swingline
Scotch
Pink Pearl

Pleasure: The Ocean

"For me, surfing is as close a connection I can have with Mother Nature. To surf, you're riding a pulse of energy from Mother Nature. And it's strong. It's real. It's there. And you're dancing with that. You're connecting with that. You might be the only person in the history of the universe that connects with that particular pulse of energy."

– Xavier Rudd

"… the ocean forces you to move more slowly, more purposefully, and yet more pliantly. By entering it, you are bathed in a grace and power you don't experience in air. To dive beneath the surface feels like entering the Earth's vast, dreaming subconscious. Submitting to its depth, its currents, its pressure, is both humbling and freeing."

– Sy Montgomery

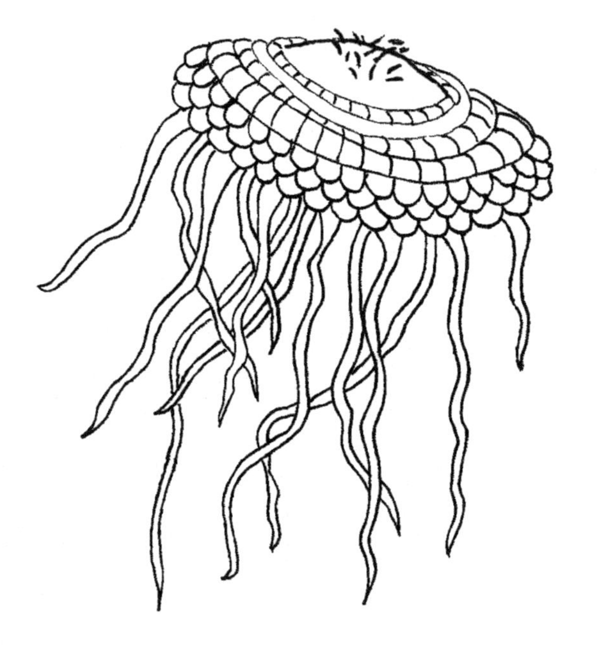

Pleasure: Kissing

"May your coming year be filled with magic and dreams and good madness. I hope you read some fine books and kiss someone who thinks you're wonderful, and don't forget to make some art—write or draw or build or sing or live as only you can. And I hope, somewhere in the next year, you surprise yourself."

– Neil Gaiman

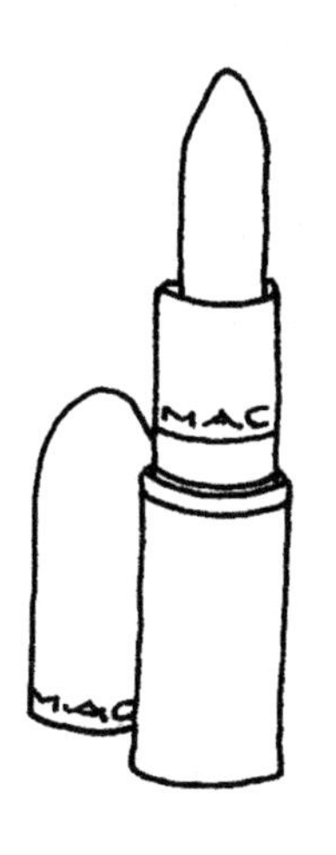

"Walk as if you are kissing the Earth with your feet."

– Thich Nhat Han

The body as a tool of connection

The mass of cells, science, and spiritual principles that we call our body is alive. We are complex super generators of sensation, energy, emotion, cognition, and intelligence. Bodies are mechanisms of engagement, the vehicles in which we participate in living. Our alive individual self only exists in connection; living is a process of engagement and exchange, whether we are aware of it or not.

Individuated and interdependent

Resilience—the ability to spring back into shape after impact, loss, and severing—keeps us alive. It is through awareness of interconnection that resilience thrives. Awareness and tuning of your whole body fully primes your engagement with the world. Yes, bodies are amazing resources for pleasure. This pleasure is important—essential even. And bodies are also hypersensitive tools of connection. Part of the joy of living in a body is not just knowing our own individual experience but also in having the capacity to be in resonance with others, to sense—through our bodies—their pain, love, and hope and how it mirrors our own. Our embodied intelligence and attunement can heal wounds.

By coloring these pages you have fine-tuned your awareness, including the awareness of your body and the priming of its capacity. Treat it like the gift that it is and share it, ensuring this magical potency continues to grow.

We encourage you to feel into the web of connections. Be generous with yourself and others. Be a place of refuge of safety and compassion because . . .

. . . you've got superpowers now!

xo,

Ray & Alex

What's the Point of All This?

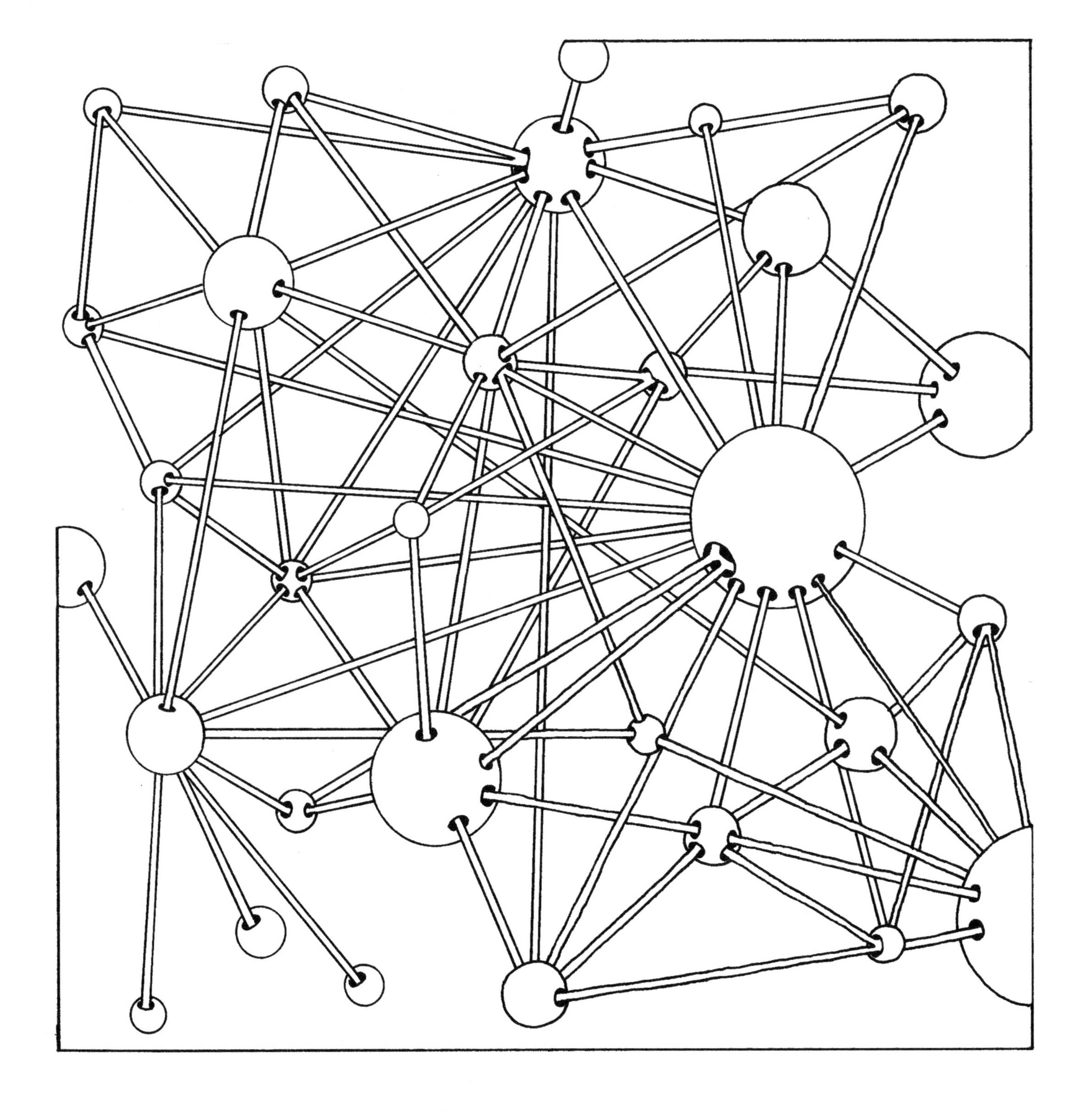

an experiment in collective coloring
First cut this page up into the puzzle pieces
Share pieces with friends to color (host a coloring party?)
Recombine to see the shared coloring beauty!
Or
You may be surprised by the synchronicities!
Color the whole image yourself first
Cut and share with 15 of your friends who have done the same
Then each of you can assemble your new coloring quilt!

This coloring book was inspired by the Beloveds—all the folks who brought their brave bodies and hearts into circles of experiment, play, and journeying with Body Trust. It was birthed out of desire to offer more people an accessible and creative way to explore our body's potential.

We want to acknowledge particular bodies and minds that deeply influenced our capacity to create. Thank you to Robert Lawrence for your ideas and innovation about senses, and Carol Queen for your energetic and seemingly endless capacity for erotic education. The world is a better place for the Center for Sex & Culture. Thank you to Zed Sinclair, our Word Top, for your excellent editing and unending encouragement. Thank you Lizz Randall, for your inspired coloring and your presence. Thank you Swami Ravi Rudra Bharati, for your teachings. Thank you Mark Fleming, for your love for poetry and a discerning Tantra mind. Thank you Jemma, our feedback diva, whose brave creativity with words showed us the way. Thank you beta readers for your careful reading and feedback. Thank you to the group of colorists who will bring the coloring pages to life with passion and excitement.

And gratitude beyond words for the collaboration and creative partnership we—Amy and Alex—have enjoyed. We used each other and those others around us to inspire a book neither of us could have envisioned or created alone.

Acknowledgements

Body Trust

Body Trust is a sacred somatic collaborative dedicated to the body as a laboratory for transformation. Founded by Alex Jade, Amy Butcher, Lizz Randall, and Zed Sinclair, Body Trust offers teachings, creative projects and workshops to inspire increased capacity for embodiment and connection in order to serve the microcosm of our bodies and the macrocosm of the planet. We honor the divine wisdom within every body's journey, the power of the erotic realm for healing and integration, and the value of access to all realms of human experience. We operate within the principles of radical inclusivity, sustainable business, circle technology, and holistic non-binary Tantra.

Amy Butcher: Designer and Illustrator

Amy Butcher is an artist, writer, facilitator, and liminal guide. She believes that play is the path to power and that the erotic is the juiciest form of play. With an MBA, M.Ed. in Social Justice Education, and diverse studies in experiential education, she brings outside-the-box approaches to group dynamics and creative projects, always hoping to midwife increased compassion through them all. Amy is also the author of the award-winning murder mystery *Paws for Consideration*. When she's not glued to a keyboard, she can be found traveling, bicycling, lifting heavy weights, or binge watching British police procedurals on Netflix. She was once described as a "silver fox," which makes her blush to this day.

Alex Jade: Writer

Alex Jade has been professionally exploring the sensate, energetic intelligence of our bodies for the past thirty years. Initially trained as a massage and movement therapist, Alex went to graduate school in social work to obtain advanced training in trauma and mental health. With clinical experience as a Emergency Department social worker and psychotherapist, she concurrently worked to develop and facilitate experiential erotic education. Alex is a student of classical Tantra, a parent, and has a deep regard for wildness. She works within the urban ecosystem by nurturing soil mycelium, hosting bees, and growing food.

We're not kidding about the circle technology thing. You, the colorist, complete us! And the bigger the circle, the better.

Let us know you're out there by sharing your finished colored images with us on Pinterest, Instagram, Twitter, and Facebook—our user name is **@bodytrustcircle**, and if you use the hashtag # **wonderbodyus** we'll see it!

If you are still curious about some of the resources that inspired us as we made this coloring book, you can find more links of interest and updates at **wonderbody.us**.

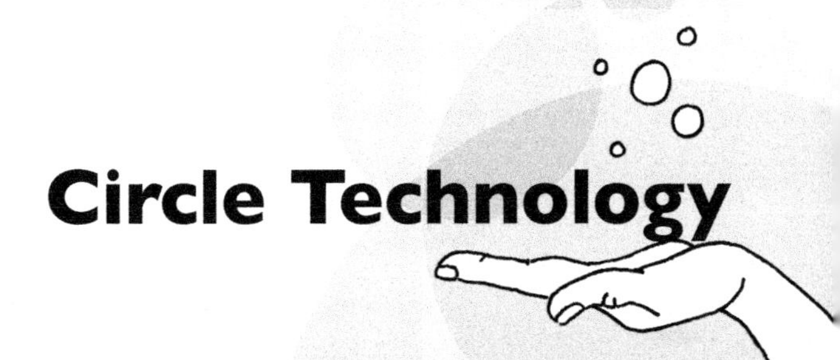

CPSIA information can be obtained
at www.ICGtesting.com
Printed in the USA
LVOW06s0316070817
544076LV00013B/156/P